W9-BET-686

SCIENCE DISCOVERY

Weather

Q&A

Janice Parker

www.av2books.com

AV² provides enriched content that supplements and complements this bo
Weigl's AV² books strive to create inspired learning and engage young mi
in a total learning experience.

Your AV² Media Enhanced books come alive with...

Audio
Listen to sections of
the book read aloud.

Key Words
Study vocabulary, and
complete a matching
word activity.

Video
Watch informative
video clips.

Quizzes
Test your knowledge.

Go to **www.av2books.com**,
and enter this book's
unique code.

BOOK CODE

S790740

Embedded Weblinks
Gain additional information
for research.

Slide Show
View images and
captions, and prepare
a presentation.

AV² by Weigl brings you media
enhanced books that support
active learning.

Try This!
Complete activities and
hands-on experiments.

... and much, much more!

Published by AV² by Weigl
350 5th Avenue, 59th Floor
New York, NY 10118
Website: www.av2books.com   www.weigl.com

Library of Congress Cataloging-in-Publication Data

Parker, Janice.
 [Weather]
 Weather Q & A / Janice Parker.
   p. cm. -- (Science discovery)
 Originally published as Weather. New York : Weigl Publishers, 2009.
 Includes index.
 Audience: 4-6.
 ISBN 978-1-62127-417-9 (hardcover : alk. paper) -- ISBN 978-1-62127-423-0 (pbk. : alk. paper)
 1. Weather--Juvenile literature. 2. Children's questions and answers. I. Title. II. Title: Weather questions & answers. III. Title: Weather
questions and answers.
 QC981.3.P367 2013
 551.5--dc23
                         2012039659

Printed in the United States of America, in North Mankato, Minnesota
1 2 3 4 5 6 7 8 9 0 17 16 15 14 13

062013
WEP040413B

Project Coordinator Aaron Carr
Designer Mandy Christiansen

Contents

What Is Weather?

Weather on Earth is driven by energy from the Sun and Earth's rotation. Weather is caused by the conditions that exist in the air at a specific time and place. All weather has four main components. These are temperature, wind, water, and air pressure. A great deal is known about the science at work in making weather, but not enough to make predicting weather patterns and events completely accurate. Weather can change without warning. It can be gentle, such as a soft breeze on a sunny day, or it can make a grand entrance, producing events like tornadoes and hurricanes.

How Scientists Use Inquiry to Answer Questions

When scientists try to answer a question, they follow the process of scientific inquiry. They begin by making observations and asking questions. Then, they propose an answer to the question. This is called the hypothesis. The hypothesis guides scientists as they research the issue. Research can involve performing experiments or reading books on the subject. When the research is finished, scientists examine the results and review their hypothesis. Often, they discover that the hypothesis was incorrect. If this happens, they revise their hypothesis and go through the process of scientific inquiry again.

Process of Scientific Inquiry

Observation
Weather can be dangerous. It is important to stay safe during severe weather events, such as hurricanes and tornadoes.

Have You Answered the Question?
The cycle of scientific inquiry never truly ends. For example, once scientists know how wind patterns affect a hurricane, they may need to ask, "Do ocean waters affect wind patterns?"

Research
Scientists use different tools and techniques to study weather patterns and severe events, including satellites, **radar**, and people on the ground tracking storms.

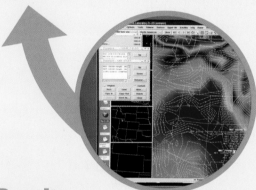

Results
Weather patterns are complex. For example, discovering how air currents, temperature, and water affect hurricane forecasts leads to more questions, more hypotheses, and more experiments.

Hypothesis
By knowing when and where a storm will strike, warnings can be issued and people can stay safe. Scientists hypothesize that early and accurate storm forecasts can help save lives.

SEVERE WEATHER

SHELTER AREA

Experiment
Scientists experiment with different ways of developing storm forecasts. Sometimes, they make accurate forecasts.

How Did People Forecast Weather in the Past?

Weather forecasting began with early civilizations using reoccurring **astronomical** and **meteorological** events to help them monitor seasonal changes in the weather. The Babylonians used the appearance of clouds to try and predict short-term weather changes. Early Chinese astronomers developed a calendar that divided the year into festivals, each one associated with a different type of weather.

One tradition for predicting the weather that has a history of success is the *Old Farmer's Almanac.* First published in 1792, the almanac gives information about weather, sunrise and sunset times, and the tides. The forecasts are given on the basis of weather folklore and a secret scientific formula. Even today, many farmers and other people whose jobs depend on the weather rely on the advice in the *Old Farmer's Almanac.*

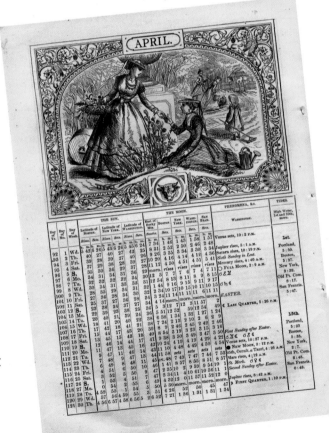

❯ The weather forecasts in the *Old Farmer's Almanac* are correct about 80 percent of the time.

Another tradition for forecasting weather that has survived from the past is using the behavior of certain animals to predict the weather. In Europe, people believed that hedgehogs could predict the end of winter. When European settlers arrived in North America, they could not find hedgehogs, so they used groundhogs instead. According to the tradition, groundhogs end their hibernation on February 2nd, signaling the end of winter. The tradition holds that if the groundhog comes out of the ground and sees its shadow, it gets frightened and runs back into the ground. This means there will be six more weeks of winter. If it does not see its shadow, there will be an early spring.

▼ Scientists who have studied the groundhog theory have concluded that this method of forecasting the weather does not work.

Digging Deeper

Your Challenge!

Research the accuracy of the *Old Farmer's Almanac* in your area. Check-out a copy of the almanac from your local library. Compare its forecasts with weather in your area. How does the Almanac's forecast accuracy for your area compare to other parts of the country?

Summary

Weather forecasting began with people using astronomical and meteorological events. Two traditions that survive today in the United States are Groundhog Day and the *Old Farmer's Almanac.*

Further Inquiry

Predicting weather is important. Knowing when the seasons will change is also important. Farmers need to know when spring will begin. Maybe we should ask:

What makes the seasons change?

What Makes the Seasons Change?

Earth experiences changing seasons. In some places, the difference between winter and summer can be drastic, from sunshine and hot temperatures to snow and ice. Other places experience less noticeable changes, perhaps only a few degrees.

Seasons are caused when different amounts of the Sun's energy reach Earth at different times of the year. Earth's **axis** is tilted as it makes its **orbit** around the Sun. When the Sun's rays strike the top half of Earth directly, it is summer in the northern **hemisphere**. At the same time, the rays reaching the southern hemisphere are more indirect. When it is summer in the northern hemisphere, it is winter in the southern hemisphere. In spring and fall, the Sun is most direct at the **equator**.

⌄ Earth's axis is tilted at 23.45° and it always points in the same direction.

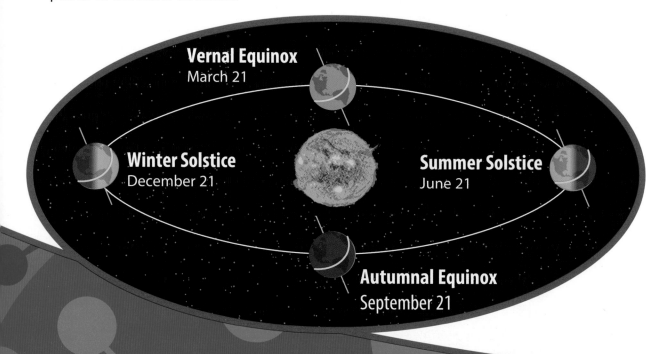

Vernal Equinox
March 21

Winter Solstice
December 21

Summer Solstice
June 21

Autumnal Equinox
September 21

Earth's Seasons

Note: the equinoxes and solstices are reversed for the southern hemisphere

Vernal Equinox
- Occurs around March 21
- First day of spring
  Every place on Earth receives about 12 hours of day and 12 hours of night. The Sun's light is spread more evenly across Earth's surface.

Summer Solstice
- Occurs around June 21
- First day of summer
  The northern hemisphere is pointed toward the Sun. Light strikes more directly, resulting in higher temperatures in the north.

Autumnal Equinox
- Occurs around September 21
- First day of fall
  Every place on Earth receives about 12 hours of day and 12 hours of night. The Sun's light is spread more evenly across Earth's surface.

Winter Solstice
- Occurs around December 21
- First day of winter
  The northern hemisphere points away from the Sun. Less sunlight hits directly and the sunlight is spread out more. This causes cooler temperatures in the north.

Digging Deeper

Your Challenge!

Poke a pencil through a small Styrofoam ball and hold it so the pencil is straight up and down. Now tilt the pencil a bit. This is how the Earth's axis is. Keep the pencil tilted and walk in a circle around another ball that represents the Sun. To see how the seasons work, keep the top of the pencil tilted and pointed at the same spot all the time as you walk. Choose a spot on a wall to help. You can even use a lamp instead of a ball for the Sun to see how light would act.

Summary

As it orbits the Sun, Earth's tilted axis changes how much of the Sun's energy reaches Earth.

Further Inquiry

The Sun's energy is important for weather, as well as the seasons. Maybe we should ask:

What is the Sun?

What Is the Sun?

The Sun is a giant ball of fiery gases 93 million miles (150 million kilometers) away from Earth. The temperature on the surface of the Sun is 10,832° Fahrenheit (6,000° Celsius). The Sun's core reaches a temperature of about 27,000,000°F (15,000,000°C). It is the closest star to Earth and one of the hundred billion stars that make up the **Milky Way** galaxy. The Sun provides warmth and light for all life on Earth. Without the Sun, the planet would freeze, and all life that relies on its energy for growth and food would die.

⌃ Scientists estimate that the Sun is about 4.5 billion years old.

❯ Just about every living organism on Earth relies upon the Sun for life.

The Sun sends out large amounts of energy in all directions. Only about two-billionths of the total output reaches Earth. This is enough energy to provide light and heat for all the plants and animals on the planet. Without the Sun's energy, the temperature on Earth would be no higher than –418°F (–250°C).

The Sun's energy arrives on Earth as different types of radiant energy, or rays. One important kind of radiant energy from the Sun is **infrared**. When infrared rays strike the skin, or any other object, the energy usually turns into heat. Nearly all of the heat on Earth comes from the infrared rays of sunshine.

Digging Deeper

Your Challenge!

The Solar Dynamics Observatory (SDO) is a space satellite designed to take images and measurements of the Sun. It was launched by NASA in 2010. Research the findings from SDO and create a picture portfolio of the images collected by SDO.

Summary

All light and nearly all heat on Earth is provided by radiant energy from the Sun. This radiant energy arrives in the form of rays. Without light and heat from the Sun, Earth would freeze. Life would not exist.

Further Inquiry

The Sun is the key to life on Earth. The Sun sends out large amounts of energy in all directions. Maybe we should ask:

What happens when sunlight reaches Earth?

What Happens When Sunlight Reaches Earth?

When the Sun's rays reach Earth, some of the energy is reflected back into space by the **atmosphere**. Most of the rays make it through where they are absorbed by land, water, or air. In the **polar** regions, however, snow and ice reflect some of this energy back out into space.

Land features such as soil, rocks, and pavement become warm when they absorb the Sun's energy. As the temperature of the land rises, some of the heat is given off into the air close to the ground. This makes the air temperature rise. Then, when the air moves, it carries the heat from one place to another.

Water can absorb a great deal of heat without showing much of an increase in temperature. When water absorbs sunrays, the energy causes some of the water to evaporate, or turn into gas, and enter the air as water vapor. This water vapor rises into the air and helps form clouds.

Water also holds onto its heat energy longer than land does. This is one reason why large lakes often do not freeze solid in winter. Since water holds heat energy well, it can also affect the climate on nearby land. Cities located along sea coasts and large lakes, for example, often stay warmer in winter than cities far from large bodies of water.

❯ In polar regions, the white surfaces of snow and ice, such as icebergs, reflect about 80 percent of the Sun's energy back into outer space.

Digging Deeper

Your Challenge!

You will need three soda pop bottles or gallon jugs, food coloring, and a thermometer.

1. Fill the bottles with water of the same temperature.

2. Place a bottle in sunlight. Place another in shade. Put a few drops of food coloring in the third bottle, and place it in sunlight.

3. Record the temperature of the water after 15, 30, 45, and 60 minutes .

Create a graph showing the temperature changes in the three bottles over the hour.

Summary

The Sun's energy may be absorbed by land, water, or air.

Further Inquiry

Earth's atmosphere traps some of the Sun's energy. Maybe we should ask:

What is the greenhouse effect?

What Is the Greenhouse Effect?

The greenhouse effect is a well-known term for how Earth's atmosphere helps warm the planet. The atmosphere traps heat near Earth's surface and keeps Earth warm, just as glass on a greenhouse holds the Sun's warmth inside. The greenhouse effect allows Earth to support living things.

As a natural part of Earth's greenhouse effect, the planet periodically warms and cools. Some people are concerned about the present warming trend because it is happening faster than ever before. **Greenhouse gases** occur naturally in Earth's atmosphere, but many human activities are contributing to higher levels of these gases. Activities that produce these gases include burning **fossil fuels**, such as oil and gas, in automobiles and jet planes.

No one can be sure how global warming will affect Earth in the future. If greenhouse gases in the atmosphere increase too much, global temperatures might rise to a level that is very dangerous. If Earth's water warms and expands, polar ice and **glaciers** could melt causing sea levels to rise. Some coastal areas would become permanently flooded. Changing temperatures could also affect crop growth, causing food shortages.

❯ The greenhouse effect is named after the greenhouses people use to grow plants in cold environments.

The Greenhouse Effect

Solar energy penetrates the atmosphere and is absorbed by Earth's surface. The heated surface then radiates some of that energy back into the atmosphere in the form of infrared radiation.

Atmospheric gases contribute to the greenhouse effect by absorbing infrared radiation produced by solar warming of Earth's surface. Greenhouse gases include **carbon dioxide**, **methane**, and water vapor.

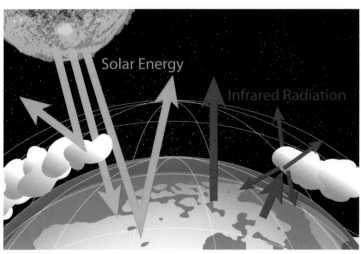

Your Challenge!

Take two bowls and place an ice cube in each one. Cover one bowl with clear plastic food wrap. Place both bowls in direct sunlight. Use a timer to time how long it takes for the ice to melt in each bowl. Which bowl of ice melted fastest? Was there a very big difference in the times? Record your results.

Summary

Earth's atmosphere traps energy from the Sun, in the form of heat, near Earth's surface. Greenhouse gases are causing Earth's average temperature to rise. This will have an effect on the global climate, as well as on people's lives.

Further Inquiry

The Sun's light arrives on Earth as different types of radiant energy, or rays. These rays create heat energy. They may also have other, dangerous effects on people. Maybe we should ask:

When are the Sun's rays deadly?

When Are the Sun's Rays Deadly?

One of the most deadly rays from the Sun comes in the form of ultraviolet (UV) radiation. Living things are protected from the Sun's UV rays by the ozone layer. The ozone layer is a layer of gas that absorbs large amounts of solar UV radiation, preventing most of it from reaching Earth.

Ultraviolet (UV) rays from the Sun can cause skin cancer, including the deadly form known as melanoma. Other effects of UV rays include damaged eyesight and, possibly, weaker defenses against infection. The United States has estimated that the loss of one percent of Earth's ozone would cause thousands more cases of skin cancer each year, and blindness in an estimated 100,000 people worldwide.

Ultraviolet radiation also harms water animals such as plankton, shellfish, and fish. Too much UV sunlight has even caused sheep to go blind in southern Chile. Some frog species could be at risk of **extinction** because UV rays damage their eggs. Crops grow smaller leaves if UV rays increase. This harms food production.

❮ There are three types of UV rays, UV-A, B, and C. UV-C rays are entirely absorbed by the atmosphere. Both UV-A and UV-B rays can cause skin damage, such as sunburns.

Digging Deeper

Your Challenge!

UV rays can be deadly. Research and answer the following questions.

1. What layer of the atmosphere protects Earth's surface from UV rays?

2. What percentage of UV rays can reach Earth's surface on cloudy days?

3. What level of sunscreen should children use to protect their skin?

Summary

Deadly effects from the Sun include UV rays, which can cause skin cancer, damaged eyesight, and a weakened immune system.

Further Inquiry

The Sun's rays bring energy to Earth. This energy is often changed into heat energy. Scientists can measure exactly how much heat an object is giving off. Maybe we should ask:

How is temperature measured?

⌃ In outer space, there is no atmosphere to protect astronauts from solar radiation. They must wear special suits to stay safe.

How Is Temperature Measured?

In the 1700s, scientists realized that water always boils and freezes at the same temperatures. This discovery helped scientists make a temperature scale to use on thermometers. The scale allowed scientists to measure temperature with the same numbers.

The German scientist Gabriel Fahrenheit was the first person to use mercury in thermometers. Mercury responds quickly to temperature changes, swelling when it gets warmer and shrinking when it gets colder. He set 0° Fahrenheit as the lowest winter temperature where he lived in Germany. Mercury thermometers are little used today because mercury is now known to be a danger to people's health.

In 1742, Anders Celsius, a Swedish astronomer, developed a scale with simpler numbers. He made the freezing point of water 0° Celsius and the boiling point 100°C. Today, his system is used around the world, especially by scientists, who find the system easier to use than the Fahrenheit method. Most countries in the world have adopted the Celsius system. The United States is one of the only countries still using the Fahrenheit system.

❮ The Italian scientist Galileo is credited with inventing the first thermometer in the 1590s.

Everyone can tell the difference between hot and cold. In science experiments, however, it is often important to know exactly how hot or how cold something is.

Your Challenge!

Not all kinds of water freeze at 0°C. Sea water freezes at a lower temperature than fresh water because salt changes the freezing point. To see this effect, fill two cups with water. In one cup add 4 tablespoons of salt and mix until the salt has dissolved. Label the cup that has the salt in it. Place them in a freezer. Wait one hour and then check on the two cups. What do you observe?

Summary

Thermometers are used to measure temperature. Most temperatures are measured using either degrees Fahrenheit or degrees Celsius.

Further Inquiry

A scale labeled with degrees is used to measure temperature. Maybe we should ask:

How is wind measured?

How Is Wind Measured?

Much like measuring temperature, the measurement of wind speed and direction is very important. Farmers, pilots, and many other professionals all need to know wind patterns and speeds in order to do their jobs.

Wind vanes, also called weather vanes, are used to tell wind direction. As wind hits the side of a weather vane, the vane is pushed around so that it points into the wind. Airports often use wind socks made of cloth to show wind direction and speed. The socks fill with air and point in the direction the wind is blowing.

❯ The highest recorded wind speed occurred at the Mount Washington Observatory in New Hampshire in 1932. The wind blew at a speed of 231 miles (372 km) per hour.

Today's weather forecasters measure wind speed with an instrument called an anemometer. Most anemometers have several cups on a wheel. This wheel spins when the wind pushes the cups around. The anemometer counts how often the cups spin, and uses this number to calculate how fast the wind is blowing.

Even without an anemometer, it is simple to tell if there is a strong wind. By observing the movements of flags, trees, and other objects outside, it is easy to see the difference between a strong wind and a light wind.

Digging Deeper

Your Challenge!

Make your own wind vane. You will need one straw, one straight pin, one index card, a pencil with eraser, and tape.

1. Cut the point and tail of an arrow out of an index card. Tape the head of the arrow onto one end of the straw, and the tail onto the other.

2. Push the pin through the middle of the straw. Stick the pin into the eraser of the pencil. Make sure the straw can turn freely.

Test your device. Can you think of ways to improve your model?

Summary

Anemometers and wind vanes are used to measure wind direction and speed.

Further Inquiry

Wind is one of the most important parts of what makes Earth's weather. Maybe we should ask:

What makes the wind blow?

What Makes the Wind Blow?

Wind is the movement of air in Earth's atmosphere. Earth's atmosphere is about 186 miles (300 km) thick. This may seem very thick, but compared to Earth's size, the atmosphere is like the skin on an apple. The atmosphere gets thinner on its outer edge. This means there are fewer particles of air higher in the atmosphere than there are closer to Earth's surface.

The wind blows for the same reason that hot-air balloons rise. Warm air rises, and cold air falls. This movement of air is wind. Ground that is warmed by the Sun transfers heat to the air. Air **molecules** move faster when they are heated, bumping into each other more forcefully. The energetic molecules push one another apart, and the air becomes thinner and lighter. This creates an area of low pressure.

Air will always move from areas where there are many air molecules, or high pressure areas, to areas where there are few, or low pressure areas. Lighter, warm air rises like a bubble. At the same time, heavier, cooler air moves in below to take its place. This causes the air to circulate. The basic rule is that whenever warm air and cool air meet, the wind will blow.

> People can use wind power to make electricity by using wind turbines.

How Wind Forms

DAY

As it rises, warm air cools and begins to fall.

Sunlight heats cool air, causing it to rise.

NIGHT

Heated by day, warm air rises at night.

Cool air descends and replaces rising warm air.

Digging Deeper

Your Challenge!

Air will always move from areas where there are many molecules to areas where there are few. To dig deeper into the issue:

Blow up two balloons. Attach a piece of string to each balloon. Use each of your hands to hold one string of each balloon so that the balloons are at nose-level, 6 inches (15 cm) apart. Blow hard between the balloons. What type of pressure system did you make, a high or a low pressure system?

Summary

Air moves upward as it is heated and descends as it cools. Wherever warm air and cool air meet, wind will blow.

Further Inquiry

Earth's spin causes the wind to blow in set patterns, or currents, around the world. Maybe we should ask:

What are air currents?

What Are Air Currents?

Wind blows around the world in set patterns. There are many elements that affect the way these global air currents move. Earth's rotation disturbs these ideal patterns. Lakes, oceans, prairies, and mountains also disturb the smooth flow of air. The Sun also affects global wind patterns.

The region of Earth receiving the Sun's direct rays is the equator. Here, air is heated, rises, and moves north or south toward the poles. About thirty degrees north and south of the equator, this warm air begins to cool and sink. This area is called the horse **latitudes**. Most of this falling air moves back to the equator. This causes the trade winds. The rest of the air continues to flow toward the poles.

Between thirty and sixty degrees latitude, the winds are called prevailing westerlies. At about sixty degrees latitude in both hemispheres the prevailing westerlies meet with polar winds called the polar easterlies. The polar easterlies form when the atmosphere over the poles cools, causing the air to fall.

> Sailors use the wind to move sailboats across water. Weather forecasts help sailors to predict wind strength.

Global Wind Currents

90°N

Polar Easterlies

60°N

Prevailing
Westerlies

30°N   *Horse Latitudes*

Trade Winds

Equator 0°   *Doldrums*

Trade Winds

30°S   *Horse Latitudes*

Prevailing
Westerlies

60°S
Polar Easterlies

90°S

LEGEND

■ **Doldrums:** calm area where warm air rises

□ **Horse Latitudes:** calm areas of falling air

■ **Trade Winds:** air blowing from the horse latitudes toward the equator

■ **Prevailing Westerlies:** air blowing away from the horse latitudes

■ **Polar Easterlies:** cold air blowing away from the poles

Digging Deeper

Your Challenge!

Test the effects of air pressure. Fill a cup one-third with water. Cover the mouth of the cup with an index card and turn the cup upside down over a sink. Remember to hold the card in place. When the cup is upside down, remove your hand from the card. What can you say about the air pressure inside and outside the cup?

Summary

Global air currents are set patterns of wind movement around the world. They are caused by the warming and cooling of air that creates areas of high and low pressure.

Further Inquiry

Winds can occur as gentle breezes or strong gusts. Sometimes, winds even forms into tornadoes. Maybe we should ask:

What turns wind into a tornado?

Q&A

What Turns Wind Into a Tornado?

Tornadoes can happen during severe thunderstorms. Only one thunderstorm in 1,000 produces a tornado. Winds inside a tornado can reach from 150 to 200 miles (240 to 320 km) per hour. Many tornadoes never touch the ground, but those that do suck up dirt, debris, and other objects. Tornadoes are very dangerous. They can lift cars off the ground and destroy houses and other buildings.

Wild winds form inside thunderclouds as warm air moves in below cool air that is moving in a different direction. Winds higher up in the cloud blow faster and in a different direction than winds below. The air begins to spin. As the air spins faster and faster, it becomes a column. The funnel of spinning air pushes down through the cloud toward the ground. This is how a tornado forms. Roughly 1,000 tornadoes occur in North America every year. Most of these occur in the United States in an area often called Tornado Alley, which includes parts of Texas, Kansas, and Oklahoma.

❯ Tornadoes begin as funnel-shaped clouds of spinning air.

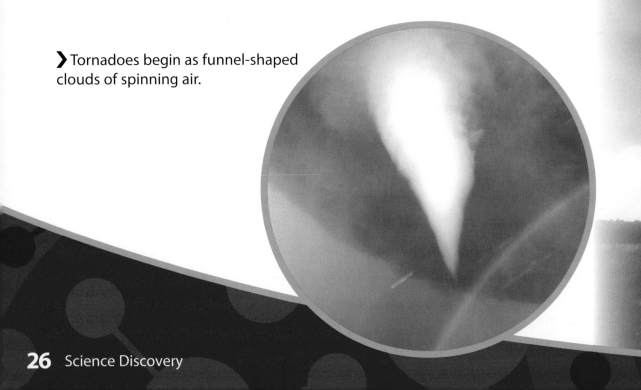

Digging Deeper

Your Challenge!

Research Tornado Alley and investigate what makes this area prone to some of the worst tornadoes ever to develop. Create a list of the five most destructive tornadoes to occur in the United States. Note interesting tornado facts as you conduct your research.

Summary

Tornados are violent wind columns that form when warm and cool air currents collide and begin to spin. Tornadoes can reach extreme speeds and cause great destruction.

Further Inquiry

Tornadoes are only one weather phenomenon that can cause damage. Another important one is called El Niño. Maybe we should ask:

What Is El Niño?

∧ The average forward speed of a tornado is 30 miles (48 km) per hour. Some tornadoes can move up to 70 miles (112 km) per hour.

What Is El Niño?

El Niño is a warm ocean current that causes changes on Earth's surface and in its atmosphere. Early Spanish sailors noticed periodic changes in water temperatures where they fished off the west coast of South America. They called the rise in temperature El Niño, meaning "The Little One" or "Christ Child" in Spanish, because it always happened just after Christmas. On average, they noted that the change occurred every few years.

El Niño is characterized by unusually warm ocean temperatures in the **equatorial** Pacific. These unusually warm temperatures cause changes in the ocean-atmosphere system in the tropical Pacific. The increased heat over the tropical Pacific results in large changes in global air circulation.

Today, scientists study El Niño events to better understand their effects on the global climate. They have found that El Niño events happen about every two to seven years. The shifting patterns of El Niño have many effects. El Niño has been blamed for everything from droughts in Africa and Australia, to floods in Ecuador, and landslides in California. Some people believe it has even caused outbreaks of tropical diseases in some parts of the world.

⌄ Droughts are extended periods of dry weather that can be harmful to people, animals, and crops.

The El Niño Event

In an El Niño event, an upper layer of warm water thickens. This thicker layer of warm water contributes to changes in global air circulation, affecting weather conditions around the world.

Normal Conditions

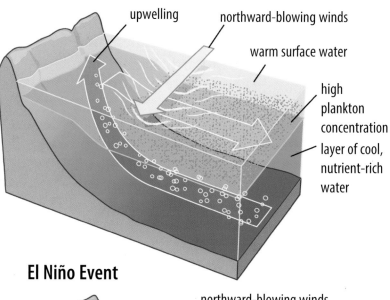

upwelling

northward-blowing winds

warm surface water

high plankton concentration

layer of cool, nutrient-rich water

El Niño Event

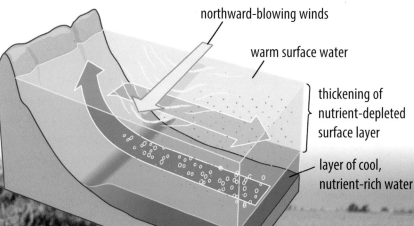

northward-blowing winds

warm surface water

thickening of nutrient-depleted surface layer

layer of cool, nutrient-rich water

Digging Deeper

Your Challenge!

El Niño is not the only weather event that occurs in the equatorial Pacific. Another event also occurs called La Niña. Research El Niño and La Niña. Then, create a chart comparing the two events and their effects on global weather patterns. Do they both cause the same effects? What are the main differences between them?

Summary

El Niño is a warming of the surface water of the eastern and central Pacific Ocean, occurring every two to seven years. It causes unusual weather patterns.

Further Inquiry

El Niño is one example of how water can affect weather patterns around the world. Maybe we should ask:

How does water affect the weather?

How Does Water Affect the Weather?

Without water, weather patterns would be very different. Water vapor in the air interacts with heat from the Sun to create weather patterns on Earth. Weather only happens in the region of the atmosphere that extends about 6 miles (10 km) above the surface of Earth. This region is called the **troposphere**. Only the troposphere contains water that has been evaporated from Earth's surface.

Water vapor is invisible, but even on a bright, clear, and cloudless day, there is water vapor in the air. When the Sun shines on oceans, lakes, rivers, and ponds, it always causes some water to evaporate. Evaporation means that water turns from a liquid that people can see into a gas that cannot be seen.

❯ When cold air moves over warm water, the air above the water often condenses into fog or mist. The same can occur when warm air moves over cold water.

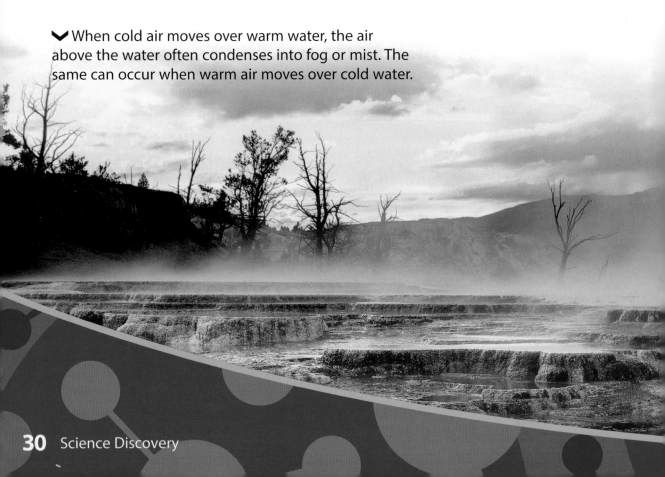

There is a limit to the amount of water vapor that the air can hold. When it reaches this limit, some of the vapor will condense, or turn into liquid. The temperature of the air determines how much water it can hold. Warm air holds much more water than cold air. For example, air at 86°F (30°C) can hold more than six times as much water vapor as air at 32°F (0°C).

Your Challenge!

Investigate water vapor in Earth's atmosphere. You will need: a glass jar, strainer, hot water, ice cubes. Fill the jar completely with hot water for one minute. Pour out most of the water, leaving about 1 inch (2.5 cm) in the jar. Set the strainer on top of the jar. Place three ice cubes in the strainer. What did you observe? Try to explain the process taking place. If you have difficulty seeing the process, shine a flashlight at different angles upon the jar and strainer.

⌄ Dew forms when surfaces near the ground become cool enough for water vapor in the air to condense.

Summary

Water vapor in the air interacts with heat from the Sun to create weather patterns on Earth.

Further Inquiry

Water vapor is an important part of how clouds form. Maybe we should ask:

How do clouds form?

How Do Clouds Form?

Clouds are made of tiny droplets of water or ice crystals in the air. When warm, moist air meets cooler air, some of the warm air cools and can no longer hold all of its water vapor. Some of this extra water changes into tiny water drops or even freezes. This forms clouds.

Clouds come in a variety of sizes and shapes. Most clouds belong to one of three basic categories—cumulus, stratus, or cirrus. You may also see the word "**nimbus**" added to a cloud name. For example, a cumulonimbus cloud is a rain cloud.

❯ People can often predict if it will rain by looking at the types of clouds in the sky.

Cumulus

These puffy clouds with flat bottoms can be as high as 14,000 feet (4,267 meters) in the air. Cumulus clouds often form on warm summer days and then disappear at night.

Stratus

These clouds form quite low and often cover the sky like a gray sheet. The clouds barely move, and the air under them is very still. These conditions can make the sky look dull and heavy.

Cirrus

Cirrus clouds are made of ice crystals. They form very high in the sky, usually above 25,000 feet (7,620 m). Cirrus clouds have a wispy, feathery appearance.

Digging Deeper

Your Challenge!

There are many kinds of fascinating cloud formations besides the three main types. For example, there are lenticular and mammatus clouds. Research the many types of clouds and create a poster presentation showing where they form in the troposphere.

Summary

When warm, moist air meets cooler air, some warm air cools and cannot hold all of its water vapor. Some of the extra water changes into liquid droplets or even freezes and forms clouds.

Further Inquiry

Rain and snow, or precipitation, falls from clouds, which are made up of water droplets. Why does rain fall from clouds? Maybe we should ask:

What causes rain?

What Causes Rain?

A cloud droplet has a million times less water than a typical raindrop. Cloud droplets are very light and tiny. Stormy air in the sky tosses small droplets around so much that they usually cannot fall to the ground. They will not fall until they collide with each other and join together to make larger, heavier droplets. If the air is very still, smaller drops may fall to the ground. This type of rain is called drizzle.

Larger raindrops usually start as ice crystals near the center of cumulus clouds. The ice crystals collect water from droplets in the clouds. The crystals grow larger and larger until they are heavy enough to fall through the air. While passing through warm air close to Earth, the crystals melt and turn into raindrops.

▼ During a large rain storm, as much as two inches (50 millimeters) of rain can fall in a single hour.

If the air temperature remains cold, the ice crystals do not melt. Instead, they fall as snow. During a severe storm, air currents may push upward so violently that they carry growing ice crystals and pellets high into the clouds. Water continues to condense on the crystals until they grow very large. When the ice balls finally fall through the warmer air below, they are too big to completely melt. They fall as hailstones.

⌄ Most hailstones are the size of peas, but some hailstones can grow as large as a baseball. Hailstones this big can be very dangerous when they fall.

Your Challenge!

A rain gauge is a tool for measuring the amount of rain that falls in a given period of time. Build your own rain gauge from an empty can or a pail. Using a ruler, measure rainfall daily for one month. Measure as soon as it stops raining. After one month, create a graph that shows the rainfall in your area. You can repeat this process each month to come up with the annual, or yearly, precipitation in your area.

Summary

Cloud droplets are very light and tiny. Rain falls when these small droplets collide with each other and join together to make larger, heavier droplets.

Further Inquiry

Rain falls from clouds. Clouds are also where thunder and lightning occur during some kinds of rain storms. Maybe we should ask:

What causes lightning and thunder?

What Causes Lightning and Thunder?

Ice particles and raindrops in clouds are made of molecules. Collisions between ice particles and raindrops break negatively charged particles, called **electrons**, off their molecules. When a particle loses electrons, it becomes positively charged. These positively charged particles cause nearby particles to become negatively charged. Positive charges collect in the top part of a thundercloud, while clusters of negative charges collect at the bottom. The ground becomes charged as well. Opposite charges attract each other with such a strong force that the charges leap from cloud to cloud or between clouds and the ground. This giant electric spark is lightning. When lightning strikes, it instantly heats the air. The quick expansion of the warm air starts a shock wave that is heard as thunder. Lightning and thunder happen at the same time, but thunder is heard later because light travels faster than sound.

How Lightning Forms

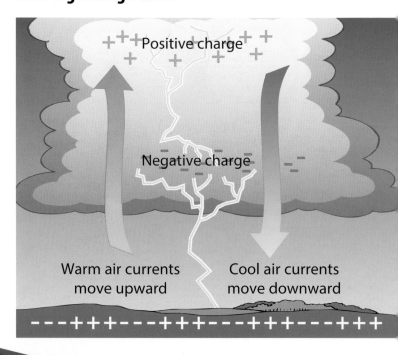

Positive charge

Negative charge

Warm air currents move upward

Cool air currents move downward

> On average, lightning strikes in the United States injure 200 people and kill 30 people per year.

Digging Deeper

Your Challenge!

There are many myths and adages about lightning and thunder, such as "lightning never strikes twice." Research more about lightning and thunder and the different sayings or stories people share that may or may not be true. Create a "myth busters" report about the fact and fiction of lightning and thunder.

Summary

Lightning and thunder are dangerous and often dramatic aspects of thunderstorms. They are caused by positive and negative charged particles leaping toward each other in the atmosphere.

Further Inquiry

Thunder and lightning often happen during violent rain storms called thunderstorms. Maybe we should ask:

What is a thunderstorm?

What Is a Thunderstorm?

A thunderstorm is a rain storm that has violent winds, thunder, and lightning. Clouds that form a thunderstorm may rise as high as 14 miles (22 km). The energy of a thunderstorm is greater than the energy of an atomic bomb. Thunderstorms often occur after a long period of hot weather. This is because the ground becomes very warm from the heat of the Sun.

A thunderstorm begins when drafts of warm air move upward, creating large cumulonimbus clouds that produce precipitation. When the cloud is high enough for the rain to begin, the thunderstorm is mature. As rain falls through the cloud, it cools the air, causing **downdrafts**. The air in the cloud becomes very turbulent, or mixed up. Finally, the rain cools all of the air in the cloud until there are no more **updrafts**. The rain stops, and winds scatter the cloud.

❮ Lightning kills more people each year than tornados do. Other dangers from thunderstorms include hail, strong winds, and flooding.

Digging Deeper

Your Challenge!

Research the stages of a thunderstorm. Then, diagram the three stages of the life cycle of a thunderstorm: towering cumulous stage, mature stage, and dissipating stage. Be sure your diagram includes the height of the clouds and how the air flows, as well as any other details you can think of to improve your diagram.

Summary

Thunderstorms occur when air near the ground becomes heated, rises, and forms cumulonimbus clouds. The storm produces violent winds, lightning, and thunder.

Further Inquiry

Thunderstorms are only one type of violent storm. An even more violent type is a hurricane. Maybe we should ask:

What causes a hurricane?

What Causes a Hurricane?

A hurricane is a powerful storm that can destroy entire cities with wind and rain. A storm can officially be called a hurricane when its wind speed reaches 75 miles (121 km) per hour. Hurricanes cause billions of dollars in damage and kill thousands of people every year.

A hurricane happens when air currents near the equator begin to circulate, and several thunderstorms are pulled together. Updrafts of warm, moist air form storm clouds, and the rain begins. The condensation of the water releases energy to strengthen the updrafts. At the top, the air moves out and begins to drop. Near the surface of the ocean, the air is drawn back toward the center. The air picks up more moisture from the warm ocean and creates more updrafts. The cycle continues, and the storm grows. As long as the hurricane is over water, it can maintain or increase its strength. When it moves onto land, it causes enormous damage to lives and to property in its path. When it runs out of water, the hurricane loses energy and dies out.

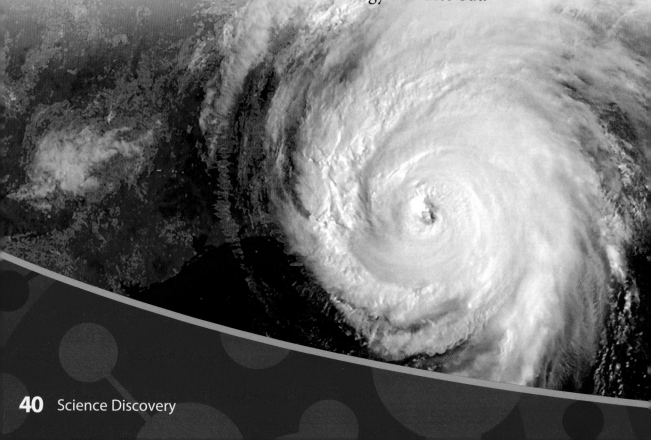

Hurricanes can cause huge, powerful waves to crash into the shore.

⟨ Hurricanes are so large, they can cover entire states and can even be seen from outer space.

Digging Deeper

Your Challenge!

Hurricane Katrina was one of the worst storms to hit the United States. It made landfall in August 2005 near New Orleans, Louisiana. Research Hurricane Katrina and the destruction it caused in New Orleans. Find out how the people of New Orleans are rebuilding their city.

Summary

Hurricanes are powerful storms that can create violent and often deadly destruction. They form over warm ocean water and strengthen into severe storms as they begin to spin, or rotate, toward land.

Further Inquiry

Understanding weather has involved asking many questions and investigating the science behind it. Taking all we have learned, maybe we can answer:

What is weather?

Putting It All Together

Most weather occurs in Earth's troposphere. Weather is driven by energy from the Sun and the rotation of Earth. Global air currents play a large part in the formation of weather patterns and events across the planet. The four main components of weather are temperature, wind, water, and air pressure. Weather conditions can change suddenly, and some weather phenomena such as thunderstorms, tornadoes, and hurricanes can be dangerous and destructive. Much has been learned about the science behind weather, but not enough to make predictions about patterns and events completely accurate.

⌄ Earth is often called the "water planet" because about 70 percent of its surface is covered with water. Most of this water is in Earth's saltwater oceans.

Where People Fit In

Everyone on Earth is connected to the weather. It affects people's lives every day. Understanding the weather and how it works has helped agriculture and other industries become more productive and environmentally aware. People are beginning to see how human activity can affect weather conditions on Earth.

The process of scientific inquiry allows scientists to study and understand the weather. Advances in science and technology allow meteorologists to predict and broadcast weather forecasts and alerts that help save lives all around the world.

Careers

Meteorologist

Meteorologists use technology such as computers, satellites, and radar to help them forecast the weather. They tell people what the day-to-day weather is and what can be expected for the next few months. They also warn people about dangerous weather systems, such as tornadoes and hurricanes.

Meteorologists research ways to prevent weather that is dangerous to humans. This includes **seeding** clouds before they become violent storms. Most meteorologists work in government offices and have degrees in meteorology.

Storm Chaser

Some people try to get as close as possible to tornadoes. These "tornado hunters" or "storm chasers" are well trained in tornado safety.

Storm chasers listen to weather reports for clues about where a tornado might happen. If a tornado appears, the storm chasers have special equipment that will help them observe the storm. Video cameras record the tornado, while other machines measure the temperature, wind speed, and air pressure inside the tornado. The information they collect is given to scientists who study tornadoes.

Young Scientists at Work

Test Your Knowledge

Test your weather knowledge with these questions and activities. You can probably answer the questions using only this book, your own experiences, and your common sense.

Fact:

Coastal areas have warmer summers and milder winters than inland areas.

Test:

You can do an experiment to show how water affects temperature. Place an empty glass and a glass full of water in the refrigerator. Wait 15 minutes. Then take the glasses out of the refrigerator. Which glass feels warmer? Look back to page 13 to find out why.

Fact:

One of the best ways to measure wind speed is by observing the effects of wind. Admiral Francis Beaufort designed a wind scale in the 1800s to help sailors judge wind speed. Today's Beaufort scale has been adapted for use on land.

Test:

Match the pictures to the appropriate wind speeds from the Beaufort scale.

A. less than 1 mile (1.6 km) per hour   D. 47–54 miles (76–87 km) per hour

B. 8–12 miles (13–19 km) per hour   E. more than 75 miles (121 km) per hour

C. 25–31 miles (40–50 km) per hour

Answers: 1. C, 2. B, 3. A, 4. D, 5. E

Quiz

Take a Weather Survey

Are you prepared for a weather emergency? The American Red Cross and The Weather Channel conducted a survey of 2,039 Americans, aged 18 or older. They were asked a variety of questions to find out how prepared people are in case of a weather-related disaster, such as a flood, blizzard, hurricane, or tornado.

Do you believe that a weather-related disaster like a flood or hurricane could happen where you live?

Would you and your family be prepared if a weather emergency happened right now?

Have you and your family prepared an emergency supply kit to get you through a weather disaster?

Do you or any family members have first-aid training?

Would you know what to do and where to go if you were told to evacuate your home?

Have you and your family ever practiced what to do in case of an emergency?

Key Words

astronomical: connected with astronomy

atmosphere: the mixture of gases surrounding Earth

axis: the imaginary line on which Earth rotates

carbon dioxide: a colorless and odorless gas

downdrafts: downward moving air in a thunderstorm

electrons: negatively charged particles

equator: an imaginary line around Earth halfway between the poles

equatorial: the regions around the equator

extinction: no longer existing on Earth

fossil fuels: fuels that come from the ancient remains of plants and animals

glaciers: a slow-moving mass of ice

greenhouse gases: atmospheric gases that contribute to the greenhouse effect

hemisphere: either the northern or southern half of the Earth as divided by the equator

infrared: invisible rays from the Sun that people feel as heat

latitudes: imaginary lines used to determine position on Earth

meteorological: pertaining to meteorology or to phenomena of the atmosphere or weather

methane: a colorless, flammable gas

Milky Way: the galaxy in which Earth's solar system resides

molecules: the smallest physical unit of an element or compound

nimbus: from a Latin word that means rain; used to describe clouds that usually bring rain or snow

orbit: the curved path of a planet, moon, or satellite around another body

polar: of or pertaining to the North or South Pole

radar: a system for determining the speed, distance, or direction of an object

seeding: adding substances to clouds in order to make rain fall

troposphere: the lowest layer of the atmosphere, 6 miles (10 km) high in some areas and as much as 12 miles (20 km) high in others

updrafts: the upwards movement of air

Index

Log on to www.av2books.com

AV² by Weigl brings you media enhanced books that support active learning. Go to www.av2books.com, and enter the special code found on page 2 of this book. You will gain access to enriched and enhanced content that supplements and complements this book. Content includes video, audio, weblinks, quizzes, a slide show, and activities.

AV² Online Navigation

Audio
Listen to section...
the book read a...

Book Pages
AV² pages directly correspond to pages in the book.

Video
Watch informativ...
video clips.

Key Words
Study vocabulary, and complete a matching word activity.

Embedded Weblink
Gain additional information for research.

Try This!
Complete activities and hands-on experiments.

Quizzes
Test your knowledge.

Slide Show
View images and captions, and prepare a presentation.

AV² was built to bridge the gap between print and digital. We encourage you to tell us what you like and what you want to see in the future.

Sign up to be an AV² Ambassador at www.av2books.com/ambassador.

Due to the dynamic nature of the Internet, some of the URLs and activities provided as part of AV² by Weigl may have changed or ceased to exist. AV² by Weigl accepts no responsibility for any such changes. All media enhanced books are regularly monitored to update addresses and sites in a timely manner. Contact AV² by Weigl at 1-866-649-3445 or av2books@weigl.com with any questions, comments, or feedback.